LICK

PHOTOGRAPHS BY TY FOSTER

KNOCK KNOCK®
VENICE, CALIFORNIA

Published by Knock Knock
1635-B Electric Ave.
Venice, CA 90291
knockknockstuff.com
Knock Knock is a trademark of Knock Knock LLC

Photographs by Ty Foster
www.tyfoster.com

ISBN: 978-160106762-3

UPC: 825703-50048-6

10 9 8 7 6 5 4 3 2 1

To my parents for letting me run around with the 35mm Nikon, and to my mentors Nikki and Rich.

LICK. As with so many great ideas—the wheel, fire, Velcro—the inspiration for this book came while working on something else. I was toiling away in the wee hours photographing dogs for a client when the treats I had began to lose their appeal with the dogs. I switched to something with a little more oomph: peanut butter (aka crack for dogs). I applied a healthy dollop to the furry models' noses, and the idea for *LICK* was born.

Like most of us lucky enough to have a four-legged family member, I've gotten countless dog kisses, both expected and . . . not so much. Even if it is kind of gross, I always close my eyes and smile as I get a full-on face licking. If you've captured such a pure moment on film, then you've surely enjoyed a laugh at the expression of the "injured" party (or parties, depending on how skilled your furry one is at doling out slobbery affection). But what about the dog? Did he too have a funny expression on his face that we may enjoy? *LICK* is jam-packed with portraits of just that.

This book isn't a serious one, and it certainly isn't an in-depth study of dog tongues. These portraits are merely meant to bring joy and happiness into your life. So please feast on the simple pleasure of dogs sticking their tongues out, licking.

—Ty Foster

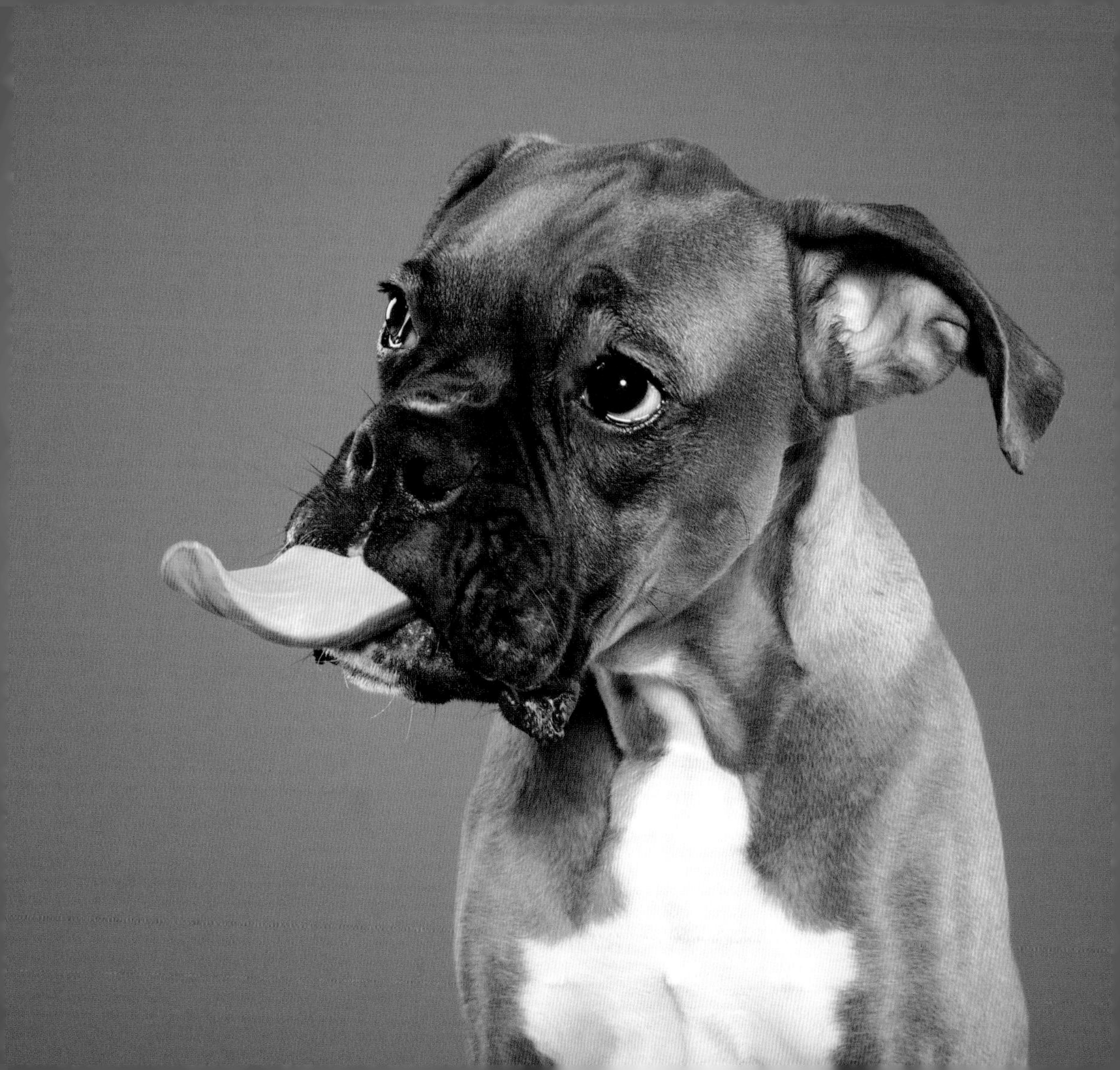

Tech
(Rhodesian
Ridgeback)

Rose
(Beagle)

Chloe
(Great Dane)

Elsa
(Mastiff)

Miss Lassie
(Collie)

Remy
(French Bulldog)

Tyson
(Chihuahua/
Dachshund)

Tuck
(Pit Bull/
Great Dane/Mastiff)

Spooky
(Saluki)

Gracie
(Rottweiler Mix)

Sissy
(Australian
Cattle Dog)

Madeline
(Dachshund)

Solo
(Weimaraner)

Cooper
(Rhodesian
Ridgeback)

Bungee
(Boxer)

Zola, Barx
(Huskies)

Fin
(Labrador Retriever)

Eddy
(Labrador Retriever/
Boxer)

George
(Pug/Bulldog)

Magic
(Boxer/Pit Bull)

Butter (Beagle Bulldog),
Skip (Boglen Terrier),
Beans (Beagle/Bulldog)

Hamlet
(Cavalier King
Charles Spaniel)

Nash
(Labrador Retriever/
Pit Bull)

Cooper
(Rhodesian
Ridgeback)

Brian
(West Highland
White Terrier)

Brutus
(Boxer)

Corah
(Saluki)

Bolo
(Siberian Husky)

Spike
(Rhodesian
Ridgeback)

Pancakes
(Boston Terrier)

Lilly
(Labrador Retriever),
Pretzel
(Dachshund)

Hans Solo
(Rhodesian
Ridgeback)

Sky
(Siberian Husky)

Freckles
(German
Shorthaired Pointer)

Crosby
(Labrador Retriever/
Pit Bull)

Cole
(Cavalier King
Charles Spaniel)

Kal-El
(Boxer)

Buster
(Labrador Retriever)

Corah
(Saluki)

Mia
(Pit Bull)

Brutus
(Boxer)

Hooch
(Mastiff)

Harleen
(Chinese Crested/
Yorkie)

Oskar
(Siberian Husky)

Manny, Carbo
(Boston Terriers)

Suri
(Australian
Shepherd)

Nica
(Brindle Mix)

Jewels
(Pit Bull)

Sheba
(Boglen Terrier)

Harry (Shih Tzu/
Yorkshire Terrier),
Pepper
(French Bulldog)

Cady
(English Bulldog)

**Stella, Cooper,
London**
(Nova Scotia Duck
Tolling Retrievers)

Arrow
(Beagle/Bulldog)

Bella
(Pomeranian)

Bella
(Pomeranian),
Molly
(Mutt)

Romeo
(French Bulldog)

Paul Anka
(English Bulldog)

Andy
(Bernese
Mountain Dog)

Carbo
(Boston Terrier)

Kelly
(Scottish Terrier)

Tonka
(Boxer)

Campbell
(Maltese/Poodle)

Pancakes
(Boston Terrier),
Stan
(English Bulldog)

Biannah
(Saluki)

Lucy
(Labrador Retriever)

Bostie
(Vizsla)

Zelda
(French Bulldog)

Lizzie
(Labrador Retriever)

Russo
(Pit Bull)

Abby
(Pug)

Boomer (Labrador
Retriever), **Chewy**
(Beagle Mix), **Sarge**
(Pit Bull/Bulldog/Mastiff)

Lucy (American
Eskimo Dog),
Teddy (Border
Collie Mix)

Milo
(German Shepherd)

Cooper
(Nova Scotia Duck
Tolling Retriever)

Rosie
(Beagle)

Freckles
(German Shorthaired
Pointer)

Coco
(Pit Bull Mix)

Charlie
(Chihuahua/
Italian Greyhound)

Teddy
(Border Collie Mix)

Buttons
(Shih Tzu/
Yorkshire Terrier)

Paloma
(Cocker Spaniel)

Nica
(Brindle Mix)

Tonka
(Boxer)

Doof
(French Bulldog/
Rat Terrier)

Marley Boone
(Pit Bull/
Doberman Pinscher)

Spud
(Cesky Terrier)

Sugar
(Boxer)

Hudson
(Bulldog)

Maggie
(Soft-Coated
Wheaten Terrier)

Penny
(Poodle)